CASTLES of IRELAND

MAIRÉAD ASHE FITZGERALD

THE O'BRIEN PRESS
DUBLIN

CONTENTS

LOCATION INDEX & MAP	4
INTRODUCTION	5

CLARE
Bunratty	10
Dysert-O'Dea Castle	10
Knappogue	12
Doonbeg Castle	12
Carrigaholt Castle	13

THE BURREN
Lemeneagh Castle	15
Gleninagh Castle	15
Newtown Castle	16

GALWAY/ROSCOMMON
Thoor Ballylee	17
Athenry Castle	19
Lynch's Castle	20
Dún Guaire	21
Aughnanure	21
Roscommon Castle	23
Ballintober Castle	23
Portumna Castle	24

GRANUAILE
Rockfleet	26

THE SOUTH-WEST
King John's Castle	28
Carrigogunnell Castle	28
Adare Castle	29
Carrigafoyle Castle	30
Desmond Hall, Newcastlewest	31
Shanid Castle	31
Askeaton Castle	31
Ross Castle	32
Listowel	33
Gallarus	34

CORK
Dunboy	36
Blarney Castle	37
Kanturk Castle	38
Mallow Castle	38
Barryscourt	39

THE SOUTH MIDLANDS

Roscrea Castle 41

Cahir Castle 41

Kilcash Castle 43

Nenagh Castle 44

Kilkenny Castle 45

Ormond Castle 46

THE SOUTH-EAST

The Hook Lighthouse 48

Slade 49

Enniscorthy Castle 50

Ballyhack 51

Ferns Castle 51

Reginald's Tower 52

THE EAST

Dunamase 54

Maynooth Castle 54

Trim Castle 55

Carlingford 56

Malahide Castle 56

Dublin Castle 58

Rathfarnham Castle 60

THE NORTH-WEST

Donegal Castle 62

Doe Castle 62

THE LAKELANDS OF BREIFNE & FERMANAGH

Parke's Castle 65

Enniskillen Castle 65

Monea 66

Tully 67

Clogh Oughter 68

THE NORTH-EAST

Greencastle 70

Kilclief Castle 71

Dundrum Castle 71

Strangford Castle 71

Narrow Water Castle 71

Jordan's Castle 72

Audley's Castle 72

Dunluce 73

Carrickfergus Castle 75

LIVING IN A CASTLE/TOWER-HOUSE 76

LOCATION INDEX & MAP

CASTLES of IRELAND

1. **Adare** p29
2. **Askeaton** p31
3. **Athenry** p19
4. **Audley's Castle** p72
5. **Aughnanure** p21
6. **Ballintober** p23
7. **Ballyhack** p51
8. **Barryscourt** p39
9. **Blarney** p37
10. **Bunratty** p10
11. **Cahir** p41
12. **Carlingford** p56
13. **Carrickfergus** p75
14. **Carrigafoyle** p30
15. **Carrigaholt** p13

16. **Carrigogunnell** p28
17. **Clogh Oughter** p68
18. **Desmond Hall** p31
19. **Doe Castle** p62
20. **Donegal** p62
21. **Doonbeg** p12
22. **Dublin Castle** p58
23. **Dún Guaire** p21
24. **Dunamase** p54
25. **Dunboy** p36
26. **Dundrum** p71
27. **Dunluce** p73
28. **Dysert-O'Dea** p10
29. **Enniscorthy** p50
30. **Enniskillen** p65

31. **Ferns** p51
32. **Gallarus Castle** p34
33. **Gleninagh** p15
34. **Greencastle** p70
35. **Hook Lighthouse** p48
36. **Jordan's Castle** p72
37. **Kanturk** p38
38. **Kilcash** p43
39. **Kilclief** p70
40. **Kilkenny** p45
41. **King John's Castle** p28
42. **Knappogue** p12
43. **Lemeneagh** p15
44. **Listowel** p33
45. **Lynch's Castle** p20

46. **Malahide** p56
47. **Mallow** p38
48. **Maynooth** p54
49. **Monea** p66
50. **Narrow Water** p71
51. **Nenagh** p44
52. **Newtown** p16
53. **O'Malley Castle,**
    Clare Island p26
54. **Ormond Castle** p46
55. **Parke's Castle** p65
56. **Portumna** p24
57. **Rathfarnham** p60
58. **Reginald's Tower** p52
59. **Rockfleet** p26

60. **Roscommon** p23
61. **Roscrea** p41
62. **Ross Castle** p32
63. **Shanid** p31
64. **Slade** p49
65. **Strangford** p71
66. **Thoor Ballylee** p17
67. **Trim** p55
68. **Tully** p67

INTRODUCTION

C astles are the most familiar medieval landmark across the Irish countryside. Sailing into view like quiet guardians of the landscape, their often romantic appearance belies their turbulent history, and their lore abounds in stories of takeovers, sieges, betrayals, and daring escapes.

Castles first appeared in Ireland with the arrival of the Anglo-Normans in the 12th century. In order to mark out and defend their new territories — great parcels of land being handed out by their king, Henry II — these invaders lost no time in casting up earthen mounds called mottes, which supported a wooden tower

on top. A D-shaped area known as a bailey was enclosed, on which domestic buildings were built. By 1200, more secure stone castles appeared, built to last for centuries. Amongst the earliest of these is Dublin Castle, begun by King John in 1204. The first fortification at Trim was erected by Hugh de Lacy. De Courcy built Carrickfergus. Castles at Maynooth, Kilkenny and Limerick all belong to the first wave of building. By 1250, Anglo-Norman knights had overrun much of the countryside, sweeping through the rich pastures of Munster where the FitzGeralds, the Butlers and the Barrys carved out lands, making themselves at home and, despite the best efforts of their English overlords, becoming fully integrated into the Irish way of life, 'níos Gaelaí ná na Gaeil féin' ('more Irish than the Irish themselves').

Meanwhile, in the southeast, where the Anglo-Normans had first entered the country, William Marshal was making a Norman imprint on the landscape with Ireland's earliest lighthouse at Hook Head, several monasteries and a string of castles and fortifications. The west of Ireland under the O'Conor dynasty, the former High Kings, was to spend several centuries fending off the Norman de Burgos.

The Black Death and the wars of the 14th century brought a halt to the first wave of castle building, but from 1400 onwards the native Irish chieftains took up the idea of building castles for themselves. Up until then, they lived as they always did, in enclosures called ringforts and the stone versions of these which were cashels, while others made their homes in 'crannógs', or lake dwellings. But now, the type of castle known as the 'tower-house' developed, being built more or less straight up and several storeys high. These are the most ubiquitous type of 'castle' visible in the countryside and, along with the earlier type, they may have numbered as many as 7,000 in the Late Middle Ages. (The terms 'castle' and 'tower-house' are often used interchangeably.) Though they more or less abandoned their ringforts for tower-houses, the Gaelic chieftains carried on in their ancient roles as patrons of the poets, musicians and scribes, and upholders of the old Gaelic order with all its rituals of hospitality and pride in past glories. Added to this were the everyday dramas of medieval life in Ireland, the running battles with neighbouring chieftains, the cattle-raiding and the disputes over succession.

However, the Tudor monarchs were determined to subdue Ireland and break the power of the old Gaelic and Norman families. This process began in earnest in the 1500s in the reign of Elizabeth I, who gave huge land-grants to her favourites, mainly in Munster, in what were known as the Munster Plantations. (At the same time, changes in warfare, especially the arrival of cannon, began to make the castle redundant and the fortified manor-house began to take its place, often built onto an older tower-house as at Lemeneagh, Carrick-on-Suir and Donegal.)

The Elizabethan Wars culminated in the defeat of the Irish side at Kinsale in 1601 and this disastrous event, followed by the exile of the Gaelic aristocracy in what became known as the Flight of the Earls, spelled the end of the old Gaelic order. The Plantation

Page 6: The beautifully restored Donegal Castle, once home to Red Hugh O'Donnell. Opposite top: Askeaton Castle, County Limerick. Above: Carrigaholt Castle, County Clare. Page 8 (inset): Carrigafoyle Castle, County Kerry.

of Ulster followed, while Plantation Castles, as they came to be known, were often imposed on the site of a chieftain's stronghold.

Cromwell's countrywide campaign of destruction in the 1640s left most of even the strongest castles ruined by being 'slighted' (making a big rent in one of the castle walls, enough to render it useless and requiring only a small amount of cannon). Many of the ruins date from that destructive period.

Today, we see a new chapter in the story of the castles in Ireland. Many have been excavated and reinstated. Some, such as Barryscourt in County Cork, facilitate research into the Anglo-Normans and certain aspects of medieval culture in Ireland. Ancient crafts have been drawn on and are being kept alive. Oak ceilings, for example, have been reinstated in many sites using medieval techniques and tools. Stonework has been restored; gardens are being developed in period style. Domestic interiors are being furnished and restored with authentic period artefacts. Much can be learned about our past from these medieval survivors.

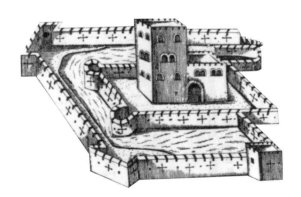

CLARE

County Clare had around 200 castles of
the tower-house type, testimony to the
strength of the great Gaelic families
of the region such as the MacNamaras,
the O'Briens, the MacMahons and the
O'Loughlins, and to their resistance to the
Anglo-Norman invaders.

Bunratty Castle, one of the most splendid in Ireland, was built to impress, its bold outline dominating the skyline as you travel westwards into County Clare.

BUNRATTY

The present Bunratty Castle, the third on this site, was built in the 15th century by Síoda Mac Conmara and later came into the hands of the O'Briens through marriage.

Essentially a large tower-house, it is one of the main tourist attractions in Ireland and few other buildings create such an impression of life in a late medieval castle. The castle came into its own in the time of the fourth Earl of Thomond, who made it his main seat around 1580, and the restoration reflects how it would have appeared in his time. Badly dilapidated by the 20th century, it was restored in the 1950s by the OPW and its owner Lord Gort, who filled the castle with magnificent medieval furniture. Today it is famous for its 'medieval' banquets, held nightly during the summer season.

The main block of the castle has three floors over the dungeons. The first floor, a great vaulted space, was where the guard kept watch. This has all the features you would expect to find in a heavily fortified medieval building: a murder-hole over the door, a spiral staircase and narrow slits of windows angled wide inside.

Above is the magnificent Great Hall where the Earl held court and dined with his guests. Furnished as it would have been in the 16th century, this room has deep window embrasures, a great fireplace and a magnificent modern wooden roof. Above are the private quarters, with the Earl's bedroom, two solars, or sunrooms, and a beautiful chapel. Bunratty has many smaller rooms, used as sleeping-quarters, tucked away in the towers and boasts no less than fifteen privies.

DYSERT-O'DEA CASTLE

Dysert-O'Dea Castle, built between 1470 and 1490, has many of the features which were a part of a well-defended late medieval tower-house. The lower floor has a murder-hole and narrow loophole windows while the pivot-holes in the walls, from which the doors hung, are visible. The top floor, with its fine cut-stone windows, is a pleasant and light living area, and from the parapets there are views over Clare to Mullaghmore Mountain. The remains of the Old

NEARBY:
Bunratty Folk Park, a living museum which celebrates everyday life in rural Ireland a century ago.

Banqueting Hall, which dates from *c*.1500, are beside the castle.

Dysert-O'Dea Castle had a chequered history, changing hands many times and becoming a Cromwellian garrison in 1651. It was regained by the O'Deas, who lost their claim to it after the Battle of the Boyne, after which it fell into ruin. Brought back to life in the 1970s, it was purchased by O'Dea descendants and restored with the help of local people.

Dysert-O'Dea Castle, 9½km (6m) north-east of Ennis, is restored and home to the Clare Archaeology Centre with its fine collection of artefacts from the Stone Age to the 20th century, and interesting audio-visual presentation. There are over 25 places of historical and archaeological interest within a few kilometres' radius of the castle.

KNAPPOGUE

Knappogue Castle is a smaller version of Bunratty. Also built by the MacNamaras and dating from the 15th century, it now hosts nightly medieval banquets in the tourist season.

NEARBY:

Craggaunowen, where a reconstructed crannóg can be seen, and also a replica of Saint Brendan's boat in which, according to legend, he discovered America in the 6th century.

DOONBEG CASTLE

Doonbeg Castle, overlooking the wide river of the same name and a fine bridge, is typical of picturesque ruins in the west of Ireland. Its ruinous state reveals the structure and layout of a typical 15/16th-century tower-house. It was the scene of many power struggles between the MacNamaras and the O'Briens before falling into MacMahon hands. A little over a century ago, as many as seven families made their home here.

CARRIGAHOLT CASTLE

Anyone who has ever heard the spirited battle-song about 'Clare's Dragoons' will be reminded of that rousing chorus on visiting the 15th-century Carrigaholt Castle on the Loop Head peninsula of County Clare. A famous regiment of horse was raised here, in the 17th century, by Viscount Clare, and fought in the armies of Europe after the Battle of the Boyne. Their ghosts are still seen on windy nights galloping along the cliffs of the Shannon estuary.

NEARBY:
The Little Ark at Kilbaha, where Mass was celebrated in defiance of a local landlord in the 19th century. Also nearby are the birthplace of the great Gaelic scholar Eugene O'Curry at Doonaha and Loop Head Lighthouse.

THE BURREN

The beautiful Burren region in North Clare is dotted with castles. Many are picturesque ruins, some are still holding out against the effects of time and weather, and others are lovingly restored as private homes and tourist attractions.

Lemeneagh Castle, the great O'Brien stronghold, was built in two parts: a tower-house (on the right) built *c.*1480 and a later fortified house, seen here on the left.

LEMENEAGH CASTLE

Visible from the roadway, but not open to visitors, this notable O'Brien stronghold was the home of the formidable Máire Rua Mac Mahon. Máire Rua was born in 1615 and, after the death of her first husband, she married Conor O'Brien, by whom she had eight children. Conor, from whom the Barons Inchiquin of Dromoland Castle are descended, was killed by Cromwellian forces in 1651. A ruthless pragmatist, Máire Rua married a Cromwellian officer called Cooper two years afterwards in order to secure the claims of her children to the O'Brien estates. She is believed to have been buried in Ennis Abbey beside her second husband, Conor, whom she claims to have always loved.

A fine gateway which stood guard in front of the castle is now at Dromoland Castle Hotel and a fireplace can be seen in the Lemeneagh Hall of the Old Ground Hotel in Ennis, with a date of 1553.

GLENINAGH CASTLE

Once home to the O'Loughlins, 'Princes of the Burren', the enchanting location of Gleninagh Castle, a few kilometres west of Ballyvaughan on the southern shore of Galway Bay, suggests that castle-builders may have occasionally chosen a site for the beautiful views.

NEWTOWN CASTLE

Built by the O'Briens in the 16th century, Newtown Castle passed to the O'Loughlins, 'Princes of the Burren'. The castle has five storeys linked by a spiral staircase. There are four machicolations on the parapets, from where intruders would have been attacked with missiles, with one placed over the doorway.

Newtown Castle was restored in the 1990s and is home to the Burren College of Art. The castle is one of only three cylindrical tower-houses in Clare and is supported by a pyramid, not unlike a rocket on its launching pad.

Notable features of Newtown are the dome vaults overhead on the ground floor and third storey and the beautifully restored conical ceiling (right) on the top floor.

NEARBY:

Poulnabrone Dolmen, Caherconnell Fort, the Aillwee Caves and the Burren Perfumery are all accessible to visitors.

MUCH OF CONNACHT WAS CONQUERED BY WILLIAM DE BURGO, AND ITS MEDIEVAL HISTORY IS THAT OF THE RESISTANCE OF THE O'CONORS – KINGS OF CONNACHT, HIGH-KINGS OF IRELAND – AND OF NATIVE CHIEFTAINS SUCH AS THE O'HYNES AND THE O'FLAHERTYS TO THE NORMAN ADVANCE.

THOOR BALLYLEE

Thoor Ballylee is a 16th-century tower-house built by the de Burgos on the Cloon river. The poet WB Yeats was drawn to this quiet area by the presence of two of his great literary friends, Lady Gregory in nearby Coole Park and Edward Martyn at Tulira Castle. He came to live here in 1918 with his young wife, Georgie, who brought great energy and creativity to making the building habitable.

'Thoor' comes from the Gaelic *túr*, which means 'tower', and Yeats's book *The Tower* (1936) took its title from this building where he spent those creative years.

One of *the* literary landmarks for the visitor to the West of Ireland must be Thoor Ballylee in the Kiltartan area of south Galway, home to the great Irish poet William Butler Yeats and his family between the years 1916 and 1928.

The place has all the romantic requirements for a poet and Yeats himself wrote of:

An ancient bridge, and a more ancient tower, ...
A winding stair, a chamber arched with stone,
A grey stone fireplace with an open hearth.

Today the tower still stands four storeys high with the floors connected by the 'winding, gyring, spiring tread-mill of a stair'. The living room where Yeats worked on the ground floor, the dining room above and the main bedroom are much as they were in the poet's day.

After Yeats ceased to live here, ownership of Thoor Ballylee remained with his family and in 1963, they placed the property in the hands of a Trust in order to ensure its restoration and maintenance.

NEARBY:

Visit Coole Park, once home to Lady Gregory. The house has been demolished, but the woods remain; the famous autograph tree which has the signatures of many of her literary friends still stands and provides a restful shade in summer.

ATHENRY CASTLE

As well as the 13th-century castle there are long stretches of the old town walls still standing, including the North Gate, one of five heavily defended entrances to this Galway town. The ruins of the Dominican Friary stand close to the castle. All this investment in building on the part of the Anglo-Normans speaks of the siege-like mentality that prevailed during their early forays into Connacht and the desperate resistance of the native population.

Meiler de Bermingham built the castle here, on the Clareen river, around 1235. The restored castle has a fine hall on the first floor with delicately carved capitals at the doorway. This was the main living area for the baron and his family, warmed by a central fire with a roof opening for smoke. The basement has a vaulted ceiling and visible traces of the wicker construction method. Two upper floors were added later and the castle probably became a garrison for the soldiers, while a more comfortable house was built in the town for the de Bermingham family.

The Athenry town walls were built in 1316 as a defence against the repeated attacks by the O'Conor kings. However, a bloody defeat for the Irish side in 1316 marked the end of the struggle to withstand the Normans, and Athenry faded in importance. The town suffered further damage in 1596 when Red Hugh O'Donnell devastated it during the Nine Years' War.

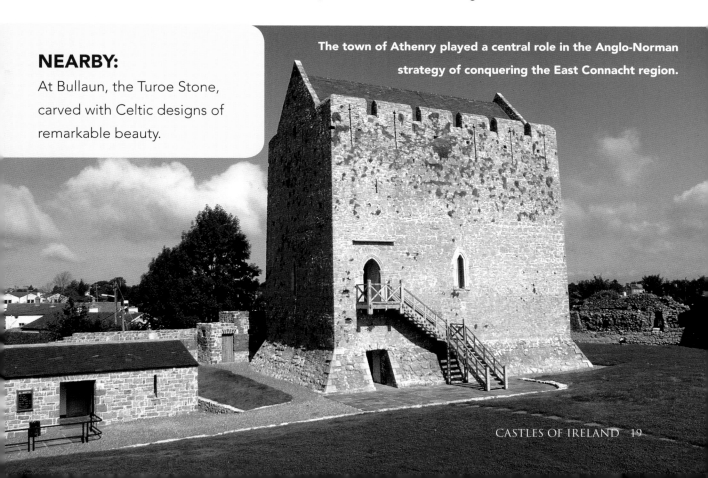

NEARBY:

At Bullaun, the Turoe Stone, carved with Celtic designs of remarkable beauty.

The town of Athenry played a central role in the Anglo-Norman strategy of conquering the East Connacht region.

LYNCH'S CASTLE

The beautiful exterior carvings on this building on Shop Street are one of Galway city's medieval highlights. The castle, in use as a bank since 1927, was built in the late 15th century by the Lynchs, a great native merchant family and one of the most influential of the Galway tribes.

Dún Guaire is a tower-house beside the delightful town of Kinvara on the inner shores of Galway Bay.

DÚN GUAIRE

Beautifully situated on a grassy knoll, Dún Guaire is almost entirely surrounded by water. It was built in the 16th century by members of the O'Hynes family, who were Gaelic chieftains in the south Galway region.

Guaire was an early king of the region famous for his hospitality, and his fort, or *Dún*, on this spot gave the castle its name.

Now owned by Shannon Heritage, Dún Guaire is another venue for banquets in the summer months.

AUGHNANURE

An O'Flaherty tower-house dating from the early 16th century, Aughnanure has two court-yards and the whole complex stands on what is virtually a rocky island with remarkable caverns underneath. The tower is six storeys high and must have been relatively comfortable for its occupants, with its fine fireplaces and wide mullioned windows on the upper storeys.

There are many defensive features: the castle has a battered base and visitors should look out especially for the murder-hole over-head just inside the entrance, from which rocks and other missiles would have been thrown down on unwelcome intruders.

A splendid banqueting hall once stood in the outer ward. The window-embrasures here have elaborately carved vine leaves and bunches of grapes.

Aughnanure – *Achadh na nIubhar* in the Irish – means 'meadow of the yew trees'.
Indeed a 700-year-old yew is to be seen on the left as you make your way to the
castle across the little Drimneen river close to the west bank of Lough Corrib.

ROSCOMMON CASTLE

Roscommon (below) was built by the Justiciar William de Ufford in the late 13th century to intimidate the chieftains west of the Shannon and extend Crown control in the west. It fell into the hands of the O'Kellys and later was taken by the O'Conors in their resistance to the Anglo-Normans. A manor-house was added by Malby, the English governor of Connacht.

BALLINTOBER CASTLE

Located just over 17½km (11m) north-west of Roscommon town, Ballintober Castle (above) is believed to have been built by the O'Conors in the 1290s and was for centuries, with many interruptions, the main seat of the descendants of this royal Gaelic family, Kings of Connacht and once High Kings of Ireland.

NEARBY:
Strokestown Park House and Famine Museum.

Beautifully located beside the waters of Lough Derg, Portumna Castle was gutted by fire 1826 but has been conserved in recent years and is of special interest for its restored gardens.

PORTUMNA CASTLE

By the 17th century, the de Burgo descendants were wealthy, influential Earls of Clanrickard. Portumna Castle, built in 1616–18 by the Fourth Earl, Richard Burke, was one of the finest residences in Ireland although never lived in by its owner. This great mansion was built at a time when the idea of the castle was changing, giving way to large fortified houses like Portumna.

GRANUAILE
(1530–1603)

GRANUAILE, OR GRACE O'MALLEY, WAS ONE OF THE MOST FAMOUS INHABITANTS OF ANY CASTLE IN IRELAND.

Carraig an Chabhlaigh or Rockfleet: located in a magnificent setting on an inlet of Clew Bay, this tower-house was home from 1566 onwards to Grace O'Malley, the legendary 'Pirate Queen'.

ROCKFLEET

Granuaile, as she came to be known, was born in 1530 into a clan who were trading and raiding for centuries along the wild, remote and uncharted coastline of the west. O'Malley strongholds were strung around Clew Bay, the deep inlets of which were to give safe haven to Granuaile in her exploits. Granuaile grew up in her father's tower-house at Belclare (no longer standing) on Clew Bay and at 16 married Dónal an Chogaidh (Dónal of the Wars) O'Flaherty who, like herself, came from a seafaring clan, whose chief exploits were raiding and plundering ships along the coast. Only the foundations remain today of his castle at Bunowen, close to the extreme west of Connemara, but it was from here that Granuaile launched her first attacks on ships entering Galway Bay on their way to the rich merchant 'City of the Tribes'.

On Dónal's death, Granuaile settled on Clare Island in her father's territory and now she was launched on her career as 'Pirate Queen'. With her loyal force of 200 fighting men she plundered and raided the coasts from Scotland to the south-west of Ireland, making her a legend in her own lifetime. Her castle on Clare Island had a commanding view and was itself almost invisible from the sea. Granuaile remarried in 1566, this time to Richard 'an Iarainn' Bourke, and from then onwards her main residence was at his castle Carraig an Chabhlaigh, or Rockfleet, which still stands today. Granuaile ran her own navy and in 1588 she captured ships of the Spanish Armada and executed the unfortunate survivors. Another claim to notoriety was her famous visit to Queen Elizabeth I. Her death, like much of her life, is shrouded in mystery, but she is believed to have died at Rockfleet about 1603.

NEARBY:

The Granuaile Centre in Louisburgh, Westport House (right) and Westport town itself, Murrisk Abbey and the National Famine Monument at the foot of Croagh Patrick at Murrisk.

THE SOUTH-WEST

THE LUSH PASTURES OF LIMERICK IN THE HEART OF GAELIC MUNSTER WERE CLAIMED FROM 1190 ONWARDS BY THE MARAUDING NORMANS SO THAT THE COUNTY HAS MORE CASTLES THAN ANY OTHER. MOST OF MUNSTER (LIMERICK, KERRY AND WATERFORD) WAS UNDER THE FITZGERALDS, WHO BECAME EARLS OF DESMOND ('DESMOND' FROM THE IRISH *DEAS-MHUMHAIN,* MEANING SOUTH MUNSTER). THE GERALDINES, AS THE FITZGERALDS ARE OFTEN CALLED, HAD MANY CHANGES IN FORTUNE AND DURING THE REIGN OF ELIZABETH I, THEIR POWER WAS BROKEN FOR GOOD.

King John's Castle, Limerick.

KING JOHN'S CASTLE

Limerick, a city founded by the Vikings, was granted a charter by King John in 1197 and because of the strategic location of the city at a crossing on the Shannon, it was decided to build a royal castle here around 1200 before King John ever set foot in Ireland. Like other royal castles, the fortifications form a rough square with a massive bastion at each of the four corners, three of which survive today. It would have made an intimidating presence on a newly constructed bridge when it was first built to threaten the local population. Even so, the castle was frequently under attack from the O'Briens and the MacNamaras, who captured it for a time in the 14th century. The castle then fell into a long decline from the 14th to the 16th centuries and Cromwell's troops captured it in 1651. Barracks and houses filled the courtyard before being cleared in the 1990s. Excavations have exposed the earlier pre-Norman occupation levels and these are visible today in the lower floor of the Interpretive Centre.

CARRIGOGUNNELL CASTLE

Although it suffered several bombardments in its long history, this Geraldine castle still makes for a dramatic sight, crowning a volcanic crag close to the River Shannon on the Limerick side, just over 3km (2m) north-west of Mungret.

NEARBY:
Cross the River Shannon and view the Treaty Stone (right). A pleasant river-side walk brings the visitor to the Hunt Museum.

One of the most romantic ruins in Ireland must be the Desmond Adare Castle on the banks of the River Maigue.

ADARE CASTLE

Adare has one of the finest collections of medieval buildings in Ireland. The castle was built in the 1190s by the Norman Geoffrey de Marisco. It then passed to the FitzGeralds, Earls of Kildare, and became home to the Earls of Desmond in the 1500s. It was lost to them during the Desmond Rebellion in 1578 after an eleven-day siege. The castle itself is a complex of buildings with a great square tower surrounded by a rampart for protection. The tower was originally on three floors with a first-floor entrance and would have accommodated the lord, his family and retinue. The Great Hall is a spacious rectangular apartment, clearly meant for entertainment. It overlooks the river and we can imagine the Earls with their advisers and guests feasting and drinking here. The castle has been restored and guided tours operate from the Adare Heritage Centre.

NEARBY:

Visit the beautifully restored Augustinian Priory in Adare, which is now in the care of the Church of Ireland. Also the Franciscan Friary and St Nicholas of Myra Church in the grounds of Adare Manor.

CARRIGAFOYLE CASTLE

In a beautiful situation on an inlet of the Shannon stands Carrigafoyle Castle, built by the O'Connors of Kerry in the 15th century. It was here at Carrigafoyle that the boom of cannon was first heard in Kerry during the Elizabethan Wars. Standing between the high- and low-watermark, the castle has five storeys and was protected by a bawn. During the Elizabethan Wars when it was in the hands of the Fitz-Geralds, whose power was being broken by the English, Carrigafoyle suffered badly, under siege for days and bombarded by Pelham, the Lord Justice, before the remaining garrison surrendered and were hanged.

Desmond Hall, as it now stands, is the restored Banqueting Hall of the Geraldine Castle which once stood here in Newcastlewest.

Askeaton Castle rises up on a rocky island in the River Deel.

DESMOND HALL, NEWCASTLEWEST

There was a castle here, at Newcastlewest, on the banks of the Arra river, from 1298 and, in the 15th century, the entire complex was repaired and extended by the seventh Earl of Desmond. He converted the Banqueting Hall from what was probably a 13th-century chapel. All we see today is the *Halla Mór* and the restored Banqueting Hall, or Desmond Hall as it is known. The rest of the castle buildings were damaged over many centuries and many wars.

Desmond Hall is a two-storey building with a small defensive tower on the north-western corner. The upper level was used for banqueting and entertainment and was reached by an outside stone stairs. The oak roof here was reconstructed in the style of the 15th century. The original hooded fireplace, dating from the 17th century, has been restored.

SHANID CASTLE

Shanid, a shattered shell perched on an earthen motte around 13km (8m) north of Newcastlewest in County Limerick, was probably the earliest Geraldine castle.

ASKEATON CASTLE

The banqueting hall in the Desmond Castle of Askeaton is considered to be one of the finest secular medieval buildings in Ireland. Built on a rocky island on the River Deel by the seventh Earl of Desmond, it stands in the outer ward of the castle. Approximately 21m (70ft) in length and 9m (30ft) wide, this was a magnificent space, with five vaulted rooms on the ground floor. The windows are large and finely carved.

ROSS CASTLE

Ross Island in Killarney, where this castle stands, has a long history. As far back as 2300BC, the island was being mined for its copper deposits, used in the making of bronze, and the way-marked Mining Trail brings the visitor on an enjoyable walk which takes in the story of the island. Try to visit Ross Castle in May or June when the woodlands are carpeted in bluebells and look out for the yew trees, the oakwoods and the famous *Arbutus* or Strawberry Tree.

The castle itself has been restored and furnished in recent times. It is surrounded by a bawn wall and has the defensive features common to most tower-houses such as the murder-hole over the entrance hall, through which missiles could be aimed at unwelcome intruders. Outside, the bartizans, or overhanging turrets, were another line of defence. Inside, the bed chamber on the second floor has a fine vaulted ceiling. Overhead is the Great

NEARBY:

Muckross House and gardens and Killarney National Park.

.

In an enchanting situation in Lough Leane, framed by the majestic mountain scenery around Killarney, Ross Castle is a 15th-century tower-house built by the O'Donoghue Ross clan, Gaelic chieftains of the region.

NEARBY:

The Seanchaí Kerry
Writers' Museum.

Listowel Castle.

Hall, the most important area of the house with two large windows and a magnificent oak roof reconstructed using the original methods.

Like most Munster castles, Ross changed hands as the fortunes of its owners waxed and waned with the events of the Elizabethan Wars in the 1500s and the destruction wrought by the campaign of Cromwell in the 17th century.

During the Cromwellian Wars, Lord Musk-erry held out in the castle against a huge force under General Ludlow. It only fell after Ludlow had a man-of-war boat transported overland from the sea and launched an attack on the castle from Lough Leane. The horrified defend-ers, on seeing a sea-going vessel bombarding the castle from the lake, took this as the deci-sive signal to abandon Ross, the last Irish castle to fall to Cromwell's forces.

LISTOWEL

Two great towers and a connecting wall greet the visitor to this 12th-century castle on the banks of the River Feale. Recently restored, it is a fine example of a massive tower-house, although only half still stands. Built by McGilli-gan, it was captured by FitzMaurice in 1582.

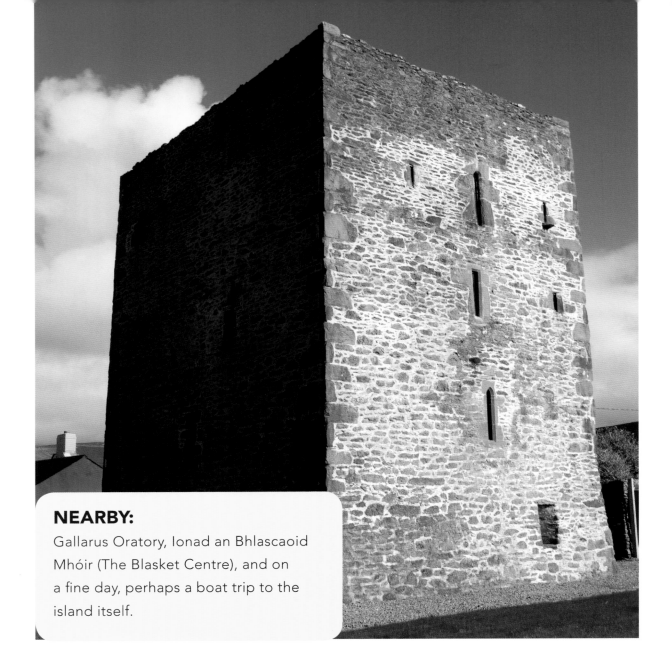

NEARBY:
Gallarus Oratory, Ionad an Bhlascaoid Mhóir (The Blasket Centre), and on a fine day, perhaps a boat trip to the island itself.

GALLARUS CASTLE

Within sight of the beautiful Kerry headland of Ceann Sibéal and close to the unique oratory of the same name, Gallarus Castle was home to a branch of the FitzGeralds, Knights of Kerry, for generations.

The story is told how the last FitzGerald to live there, an old man fiercely proud of his family's resistance to the English, lay dying of extreme old age. As a great storm raged outside, he revived and asked to be carried to the window from which he could watch the fury of the storm raging across Smerwick Harbour. His last words were: 'Tis just the day for a Geraldine to die.'

CORK

HISTORY CLINGS TO THE WALLS AND BATTLEMENTS OF THE MANY RUINED CASTLES IN WEST CORK LINKED TO IRISH FAMILY NAMES LIKE O'SULLIVAN AND MACCARTHY. PLACE NAMES SUCH AS KINSALE, BANTRY BAY AND DUNBOY STILL CARRY THE ECHOES OF HISTORY. THE MOST DECISIVE BATTLE EVER FOUGHT IN IRELAND TOOK PLACE AT KINSALE IN 1601. THE DEFEAT OF THE IRISH THAT DAY CHANGED FOREVER THE OLD GAELIC ORDER. (VISITORS CAN SEE THE STAR-SHAPED FORT AT KINSALE WHICH WAS A FORTIFICATION TYPE OF THE 17TH CENTURY AND SUPERSEDED THE TOWER-HOUSE FOR DEFENCE PURPOSES.)

A grassy ruin is now all that remains of the great stronghold of Dunboy which lies opposite Bere Island on the rugged Beara peninsula.

DUNBOY

The Irish writer Seán Ó Faoláin calls Dunboy 'one of the great reverberations of the awful downfall at Kinsale'. After the defeat, the rampaging English army under Sir George Carew carried on the war and laid siege to Dunboy on the Beara peninsula, stronghold of the chieftain Dónal Cam O'Sullivan Beare. The brave garrison withstood the siege for several weeks and when the commander, MacGeoghegan, seeing all was lost, was about to torch a pile of gunpowder and blow up his own men along with the enemy, he was cut down and the rest of the garrison unmercifully executed.

What followed gave rise to one of the most dramatic stories of endurance to come down to us. O'Sullivan Beare himself, having held out in the mountains, gathered his followers, about 1,000 people, and set out on 31 December 1602 on a brave and desperate march northwards to O'Rourke's castle in Leitrim, in order to join up with Hugh O'Neill, commander-in-chief at Kinsale. The ragged band was ambushed and harried every step of the way and this, along with the snows of winter and the difficult terrain, resulted in unimaginable hardship. On reaching the Shannon they killed the horses in order to make skin boats. By the time they reached Leitrim, on 14 January 1603, only around 35 people had survived.

The end of the Nine Years' War came soon afterwards with O'Neill's surrender to the Queen's Deputy. For Dónal Cam there was no going back. He was part of the great lamented exodus of chieftains as he sailed for Spain, where he lived for many years before being accidentally stabbed to death.

Dónal Cam was succeeded as chieftain of Beara by his cousin Owen, known as the Queen's O'Sullivan.

'All Blarney!' shouted Elizabeth I when she heard the latest reports of Cormac MacCarthy, Lord of Muskerry, whose main castle was at Blarney. He was renowned for his silvery tongue and the ability to please all sides in an argument. The queen's remark is said to have started the tradition that 'the gift of the gab' can be yours by visiting his castle at Blarney, one of the most famous in Ireland. Thus, visitors who kiss the famous stone (right) can hope to acquire the gift of eloquence.

Blarney Castle was probably built in 1446 by an earlier Cormac Mac Carthy, Lord of Muskerry, known as Cormac Láidir (The Strong). Blarney is a mighty five-storey tower, with a cylindrical building added to the front in the 18th century.

BLARNEY CASTLE

Blarney Castle, in County Cork, has some fine defensive features such as the machicolations and battlements which still manage to look threatening today. Cromwell's ubiquitous forces captured the castle in 1646, but it was returned to the MacCarthys less than twenty years later at the Restoration. Even though the MacCarthys lasted longer than many great Gaelic chieftains, their days as Lords of Muskerry were over and the castle entered a new phase of life when it was acquired by the English Sir James Jefferyes after the defeat at the Boyne in 1691.

KANTURK CASTLE

Kanturk Castle, situated about 19km (12m) west of Mallow, is a Jacobean semi-fortified house dating from 1610. It is unusual in that it was built by a native Munsterman, Dermot MacDonagh. However, it was never completed, as Planter neighbours, fearful of the native population, caused the building to be stopped.

MALLOW CASTLE

Mallow Castle on the River Blackwater, another fortified house, was built around 1593 by an English Planter, Sir John Norreys, on the site of an old Desmond fortress.

Just east of Cork city beside the village of Carrigtwohill, Barryscourt reveals how life was lived by the occupants in the 16th century. High tides came close to the walls and we can imagine approaching the castle by boat.

The interior of Barryscourt.

NEARBY:
Fota House, the Arboretum and
Fota Wildlife park.

BARRYSCOURT

The Barrys came to Munster with the Anglo-Normans in the 12th century and the tower-house at Barryscourt was the main seat of the family in the 15th and 16th centuries. Inside the main entrance a murder-hole allowed the guard to monitor all visitors.

The Great Chamber, the principal room of the castle, is spacious and light with a large fireplace inscribed with the date 1588. Stone corbels set into the walls would have supported a gallery. Both this room and the vaulted room on the first floor are furnished and reinstated as a domestic interior. Furniture, drinking vessels and tableware in the style of the 16th century are displayed, suggesting the hospitality and entertainment for which Irish castles were famous. Of great interest is the chapel as these were common in Anglo-Norman castles and rare in tower-houses such as Barryscourt. The visitor should look out for fragments of painted plaster which still survive on the walls and ceiling.

Outside, we can inspect the bawn, the wall of which would have enclosed a range of wooden buildings, including a large hall which probably served as a kitchen. There were gardens too in the 16th century; a herb garden has been reinstated in the bawn.

THE SOUTH MIDLANDS

MUCH OF THE LAND OF PRESENT-DAY TIPPERARY AND KILKENNY, TERRITORY OF GAELIC FAMILIES SUCH AS THE O'BRIENS, O'KENNEDYS AND O'CARROLLS, CAME INTO THE HANDS OF THE BUTLERS, LATER DUKES OF ORMOND (FROM THE IRISH *OIRMHUMHAIN* = EAST MUNSTER).

Roscrea Castle makes an interesting medieval focus in the centre of town. Just outside the medieval walls lies a very attractive formal garden.

ROSCREA CASTLE

Roscrea was a royal castle, heavily defended and, due to its proximity to the mines at nearby Silvermines, of great strategic importance. A motte and bailey here gave way to the stone-built castle around 1280 when silver was discovered at the mines. The castle became the property of the Butlers in 1315 and consists of a massive gatehouse and a large walled enclosure. The gatehouse is of special interest with its drawbridge and portcullis (lifting gate). Visitors can examine the reconstructed mechanisms for lifting these on the first floor. The basement housed a prison, and a spiral staircase brings us to the first and second floors where the main rooms are. There are several passages and small rooms off these main chambers, where soldiers and household staff slept as best they could.

Standing within the castle yard is Damer House, which dates from around 1720. Three storeys over a basement, it has a very fine carved timber staircase.

NEARBY:

The Heritage Centre beside the round tower. The ornate façade of the 12th-century Romanesque church. The ancient Romanesque church and High Cross at Monaincha two miles south-east of Roscrea.

CAHIR CASTLE

An earlier stone fortification, or *cathair*, belonging to the O'Briens stood here before the Anglo-Norman Philip of Worcester arrived in the 13th century, banished the O'Briens and built the earliest castle on the site. The Butlers, Earls of Ormond, were in possession from 1375

Standing on a rocky island in the River Suir, the layout of Cahir Castle looks much as it did in 1599 when it was illustrated in *Pacata Hibernia*. The present town of Cahir grew up around the castle since this map was drawn.

Cahir Castle.

and building went on throughout the 15th and 16th centuries. An important castle, it was battered by artillery for two days in 1599 during the Elizabethan Wars and Cromwell besieged it in 1650.

The castle consists of three courtyards, or wards, an inner, middle and outer with the core buildings in the inner ward. The reception area today admits us to the small middle ward. On our right the massive three-storey keep is the main building in the castle and the most complete early structure. A notable feature here is the gateway into the inner ward which is protected by a portcullis, a lifting iron gate with double machicolations overhead. The restored portcullis machinery is in working order and can be viewed in the room overhead.

Within the inner ward there is the restored Hall and two towers, one at each of the northern corners. The Hall is where the lord would have entertained his most important guests. The west wall belongs to the original building. The large outer ward was constructed in the 16th century and a house, Cahir Cottage, was built at the far end in the 19th century. It houses an audio-visual exhibition today.

KILCASH CASTLE

An air of poignancy hangs over this Butler tower-house, which has come to symbolise the passing of the old Gaelic and Anglo-Norman order. The old song goes, *'Cad a dhéanfaimíd feasta gan adhmad?/ Tá deireadh na gcoillte ar lár,'* which translates as 'What will we do now for timber?/The last of the woods are down.' Set against the romantic background of Sliabh na mBan, not far from Clonmel, Kilcash is today a picturesque and symbolic ruin, best viewed from a distance as the building is unsafe.

NENAGH CASTLE

In the original Nenagh Castle complex, the keep was joined by curtain-walls to four small towers and a gatehouse, all enclosing a courtyard. Theobald FitzWalter, ancestor of the Butlers, Dukes of Ormond, commenced building here in 1200. The keep was four storeys in height and today has several good examples of the defences of medieval buildings: the walls of the keep have a batter and a fine machicolation at third-floor level. The original doorway was on the first floor and the first and second storeys have arrow-slits with deep embrasures. By contrast, the third floor features some of the comforts of life: light floods in through four windows; there is a fireplace and a garderobe. The castle has been restored and is open to the public.

Below: The distinctive circular keep of Nenagh Castle stands over 30.5m (100ft) high, crowned by crenellations installed in 1861.

KILKENNY CASTLE

Probably begun by William Marshal, the plan of Kilkenny Castle is basically three main blocks (originally four), linked by three massive corner-bastions dating from the 13th century. The castle came into Butler hands in the late 14th century, when it became the main seat of this powerful family, the Earls and later Dukes of Ormond. Badly damaged in the Cromwellian Wars, it was reconstructed and remodelled more than once, the second time in an attempt to restore its medieval character. The great picture-gallery, lined with portraits and other paintings of historical interest, was built in the 1850s to the design of Benjamin Woodward. The castle remained in Butler hands until 1967, when it was transferred to the State.

The medieval city of Kilkenny preserves many buildings from the Middle Ages. The River Nore flows through it and along its banks, set in formal parkland, is Kilkenny Castle, another Ormond stronghold that was in Butler hands for over 500 years.

NEARBY:

St Canice's Cathedral, Dame Kyteler's House in the city and Jerpoint Abbey near Thomastown.

A beautifully proportioned and harmonious building, Ormond Castle has a pleasing façade with its mullioned windows, while the interior is embellished with lavish plasterwork.

ORMOND CASTLE

Ormond Castle in Carrick-on-Suir comprises part of a 15th-century tower-house with a built-on Tudor manor house. It was the best example of its kind to be built in Ireland. During the 16th century, style was replacing defence in architecture, so the murder-holes, the machicolations and the guard-rooms went out of fashion.

The house was built under 'Black Tom' Butler in the reign of Elizabeth I. Black Tom was brought up in the English court and was *au fait* with modern English court society. He was devoted to his queen, who was also his cousin, and had great hopes that she would visit his home in Carrick, but such a visit never came to pass. Indeed tradition tells us of a belief that Anne Boleyn, mother of Queen Elizabeth, was born here.

Mural paintings of Black Tom and Queen Elizabeth greet the visitor in the hallway. Of great interest are the historical documents on display. But the most memorable feature of the house is the 19m (63ft) long gallery on the first floor. Light-filled and airy, it has a richly moulded plastered ceiling, embellished with the arms of the Ormonds. An inscription on the very grand limestone fireplace states that it was erected in 1565. Up above are the attics, surprisingly light and spacious with beautifully restored timberwork.

THE SOUTH-EAST

The open sea is ever present here in this corner of Ireland. Its great natural harbours attracted the earliest Anglo-Normans, who first set foot in Ireland at Bannow Bay in Wexford in 1169. One of the most energetic and ambitious of the knights to arrive was William Marshal and he quickly set about exploiting the strategic importance of the fine coastline. He founded the town of New Ross at the confluence of the Barrow and the Nore, built a string of fortifications and castles and founded monasteries.

THE HOOK LIGHTHOUSE

A fifth-century monk, Saint Dubhán, established a continuous fire at Hook Head (*Dubhán* = Hook) in order to warn mariners of the perils of the sea. The present tower was built there for the same purpose in the early 12th century by William Marshal. As a building, Hook has many of the attributes of a castle and Marshal modelled its cylindrical shape on the circular castles he would have seen in France. He had also been on the Crusades to the Holy Land and would have seen lighthouses on the shores of the Mediterranean, probably at Alexandria in Egypt.

Monks from a nearby monastery lived in the lighthouse and manned it for almost 400 years. Their main task would have been keeping alight the fire, which blazed night and day from the top of the tower as a guide to ships entering Waterford Harbour. A small chapel stood at the foot of the tower and the interior is indeed like any fortified building with its winding mural staircase, its narrow slit windows and massive walls.

In 1791, the fires on top of the tower were replaced by more reliable whale-oil lamps and today an automated light still beams out, replacing the generations of keepers and their families who lived here. Information on the whole area of the Hook is exhibited in the visitor area.

SLADE

Within sight of the Hook, Slade tower-house dominates a tiny harbour. It probably dates from the late 15th century with a later hall attached. The main chamber is on the third floor and has two windows and a fireplace. Owned by the Laffans, a native Irish merchant family in late medieval times, it was forfeited by them in the 1641 Rebellion.

Enniscorthy Castle now houses the Wexford County Museum.

ENNISCORTHY CASTLE

The Norman knight Philip de Prendergast built an early castle here. He was drawn by the dense oak forests which covered the region (known as the Duffry from *Dubh-Thír*, which means 'black country', so called because it was black with oak) and the strategic advantages of a tidal river, the Slaney. As happened elsewhere in the 14th century, the Irish fought back and the castle was in the hands of the MacMurrough Kavanaghs for the next century. It was taken into Crown possession during the reign of Elizabeth I and granted to Sir Henry Wallop, an entrepreneurial Planter who exploited the forests of Leinster and exported them through the Slaney.

BALLYHACK

The picturesque village of Ballyhack at a ferry crossing to Passage East is home to a small tower-house (right), built *c.*1450 by the Knights Hospitallers of St John, a great military order associated with the Crusades in the Middle Ages.

FERNS CASTLE

Built on the site of an earlier castle by William Marshal the younger in the early 1200s, Ferns Castle changed hands many times. Captured by the Irish, it was in the hands of the Kavanaghs from 1360–1539. Burned in 1577, it was rebuilt in 1607 only to be surrendered to Cromwell's general, Coote, in 1641. The great rock-cut moat, which enclosed the castle, is visible today and you can also see the remains of the gatehouse and the drawbridge near the south-west tower. Three storeys high, the chambers were vast and imposing, with those on the upper storey lit by pairs of fine trefoil-pointed windows. The beautiful circular chapel in the south-east tower is the most remarkable feature of the castle with moulded rib-vaulting and floral carvings.

Ferns Castle belongs to a type of castle which has a massive keep, or tower, with a round tower at each corner.

NEARBY:
The fine museum housing the treasures of Medieval Waterford.

REGINALD'S TOWER

Sturdy and uncompromising, this fine tower has stood guard here as part of the medieval defences of the city of Waterford for over 800 years. Part of a circuit of walls and towers built by the Anglo-Normans, the tower stands on the site of an earlier Viking stronghold and bears the name of Regnall, whose Viking grandfather, Ivor the Boneless, founded the city.

The tower has four storeys linked by a spiral staircase and is home to a fine museum which explores the story of the building and the role of the city's defences. Reginald's Tower has had many roles in its long lifetime and was, at various times, used as a mint, a prison and an arsenal.

THE EAST

THE ANCIENT LANDS OF MEATH, LOUTH, DUBLIN AND KILDARE WERE COLONISED EARLY IN THE ANGLO-NORMAN INVASION, WHILE THE PALE, THE ENGLISH ADMINISTRATIVE REGION AROUND DUBLIN, WAS DENSE WITH CASTLES.

Anyone climbing the Rock of Dunamase in County Laois is rewarded with magnificent views. An Irish fort stood here on the massive rock before it was granted to the Anglo-Norman Strongbow on his marriage to Aoife, the daughter of Dermot MacMurrough.

DUNAMASE

Dunamase came into the hands of William Marshal by marriage and, as he did elsewhere, he left his mark on the landscape. An enormous rectangular tower was built on the hill, making this a mighty stronghold with views over the pass into the west Wicklow hills.

The walls of the inner bailey have a gateway on the eastern side, flanked by towers which contain the guardrooms. It is easy to imagine the clatter of hooves and the shouts of determined knights on horseback here. Excavation work in the 1990s showed that this castle was a powerful stronghold with its own ironworks on the site, where arrowheads, horse equipment, locks and keys and all the paraphernalia of medieval warfare were made. Medieval pottery for use in the castle was made on the site also, suggesting a self-sufficient and well-run household.

Dunamase was captured by the O'Mores in the 14th century, and was in their hands until 1641 when it was taken by the English. The site is sadly a ruin since the Cromwellians blew it up in 1650.

MAYNOOTH CASTLE

Built in 1210, Maynooth Castle stands on the site granted to Gerald FitzMaurice by Strongbow at the junction of the Lyreen river and a small tributary. The great keep and the gatehouse still remain, along with some of its eastern walls and towers.

The castle, as home to the King's Lord Deputy, was the centre-point of the Kildare influence until the decline in the FitzGerald fortunes under the Tudor monarchs.

The all-powerful Earls of Kildare had their chief residence at Maynooth Castle from the early 14th century to the 16th.

The massive keep of Trim Castle stood in a walled area of 1.5 ha. (3 acres). The walls were protected by the river and a water-filled moat, while towers and gatehouses made them impregnable to attack.

TRIM CASTLE

Most of the ancient kingdom of Mídhe, which includes modern County Meath, was granted to the powerful and ambitious Hugh de Lacy in 1172 and here on the banks of the River Boyne, the most celebrated river in Irish mythology, and some miles upstream from Newgrange, he built the largest Anglo-Norman castle in the country. An ancient crossing on the river gave the name *Áth Troim* ('the ford of the elder trees') to the place. Trim Castle was an abode of great grandeur and importance, de Lacy being Lord Justiciar of Ireland.

The main chambers in the keep are enormous spaces suitable for public gatherings such as parliaments, feasts and courts with the residential quarters in the towers. The chapel, as was usual in most castles, is in the east tower and, by contrast with the other areas of the keep, is small in scale. Trim Castle was a hive of activity. Seven parliaments were held here. As well as the keep, houses, stables and a Great Hall stood here within the walls.

CARLINGFORD

Carlingford Castle in northern County Louth stands guard over a natural harbour on the south side of a deep sea lough of the same name. Around 1200, Hugh de Lacy chose this site for its strategic importance. King John's Castle is best appreciated when viewed as part of the medieval town which grew up around it, with its narrow streets, defensive walls, the Friary and the town-houses of rich merchants. Carlingford is also an ideal starting point for an exploration of the historical Cooley peninsula with its Táin Trail.

MALAHIDE CASTLE

Malahide Castle, surrounded by parklands and woods, lies 14.5km (9m) north of Dublin. Home to the Talbot family since the 12th century, it was bought by the State in 1976.

An ancient tower-house forms the core of Malahide Castle and the corner-towers along with the entrance hall are 18th-century additions. The drawing rooms and various bedrooms are all of great interest, furnished as they would have been by a family who had deep roots here. Furniture, portraits and oak-panelled rooms all convey a sense of the history of this place and indeed of the history of Ireland.

The castle has no shortage of ghostly traditions. The White Lady, as she came to be known, steps out of a picture and glides around the castle in the depths of the night. Another restless ghost is said to be Puck, a tiny caretaker who makes his home in a turret close to the Great Hall. He takes his duties as sentry very seriously and is known to have appeared unexpectedly in photographs.

The Oak Room with its 16th-century panelling is built into the remains of the old tower-house and is dominated by a magnificent carved fireplace.

The 260-acre demesne, now a public park, contains world-famous gardens.

The Great Hall at Malahide Castle retains its medieval character. At one end of the room is an enormous painting of the Battle of the Boyne, at which the Catholic Talbot family fought on the Jacobite side. No less than 14 members of the family were killed in that battle.

Dublin Castle was the centre of power in Ireland and symbol of English rule up to the foundation of the Irish Free State in 1922. Today the castle hosts state occasions, official tribunals, presidential inaugurations, European Union meetings and conferences, and is home to the Chester Beatty Library and a Garda museum.

DUBLIN CASTLE

The building of Dublin Castle started in 1204, when King Henry II ordered Meiler Fitz Henry to build a castle to defend the city, hold his treasure, and administrate his new colonial territories. Dublin was already an important Norse city, and the new royal castle was well placed to oversee the regulation of trade and commerce.

Originally a rectangular area surrounded by walls with a strong bastion at each corner, the castle walls were washed by the River Poddle on two sides and boats could come from the Liffey to a pool on the south side where the

Castle Gardens are today. Known as *Dubhlinn* or 'dark pool', it gave its name to the city. A moat was formed from the diverted river on the two other sides. The Record Tower is the most complete medieval corner tower to survive, though remodelled in the 19th century, while the base of the Bermingham Tower is original and can be viewed on the south side of the complex close to the Chester Beatty Library. The Powder Tower was excavated in 1980 when the massive bastion at the base came to light. This can be viewed as part of the display today in the Undercroft. The excavations also revealed layers of Viking activity, demonstrating that the tower was built on centuries of Viking settlement.

The castle came into its own as the centre of English government and administration in Ireland during the 16th century in the reign of Elizabeth I, when Ireland was subjected to a policy of total conquest and religious persecution. It was a prison too, amongst its many roles, where torture and hardship were the order of the day.

The long journey towards Irish independence was mirrored here in Dublin Castle. Robert Emmet, leader of the abortive 1803 Rising, had planned to seize Dublin Castle, but was captured and brought here, before being court-martialled and condemned to be hanged.

During the First World War, the State Rooms were turned into a hospital for wounded soldiers and in 1916, many of the dead and wounded from the Easter Rising were brought here. Amongst them was the badly injured James Connolly, who was court-martialled and condemned to death from his bed in the State Apartments. The room he occupied is now known as the James Connolly Room.

During the War of Independence, the Castle, which was the headquarters of British Administration in Ireland, was infiltrated by Michael

The young Red Hugh O'Donnell was kidnapped in 1587 and held at Dublin Castle. He made a daring escape only to be recaptured and held in the massive Record Tower, (on the right of picture). His second escape, in the winter snows of 1592, became the stuff of legend. The building on the left houses the Chester Beatty Library.

Collins's information-gathering network and was the nerve-centre of his activities as Director of Organisation and Intelligence of the IRA. One of the most dramatic moments in the long history of the Castle took place in 1922 when Collins, on behalf of the new Irish Government, received the handover of the castle. He marvelled at 'that dread Bastille of Ireland' being formally surrendered into his hands by the Lord Lieutenant in the Council Chamber.

Built in 1583 by Adam Loftus, Rathfarnham was designed as a comfortable country residence, but is in fact a defensive structure with a tower at each corner.

RATHFARNHAM CASTLE

Much of the interior of Rathfarnham Castle reflects 18th-century renovations done by Henry Loftus. Highlights are the splendid ceilings on the first floor and fine rococo stucco work in the ground-floor library. The artist Angelica Kauffmann visited in the 18th century and painted a family portrait, now in the National Gallery of Ireland. The castle had its resident ghost, a phantom dog, which drowned while trying to save his master and whose ghostly howls were often heard on windy nights. Another uneasy soul walked at night, a young woman whose mummified remains were discovered behind a panel in the upstairs octagonal room.

THE NORTH-WEST

The ancient territory of the O'Neills, the O'Donnells and the Maguires, Ulster resisted the Anglo-Norman conquest for centuries. But after the disastrous defeat of the Irish at Kinsale in 1601, the lands and property of the defeated chieftains were shared out to newcomers from Scotland in what was known as the Ulster Plantation. Plantation Castles were built on these confiscated lands, often on the location of a former Gaelic stronghold.

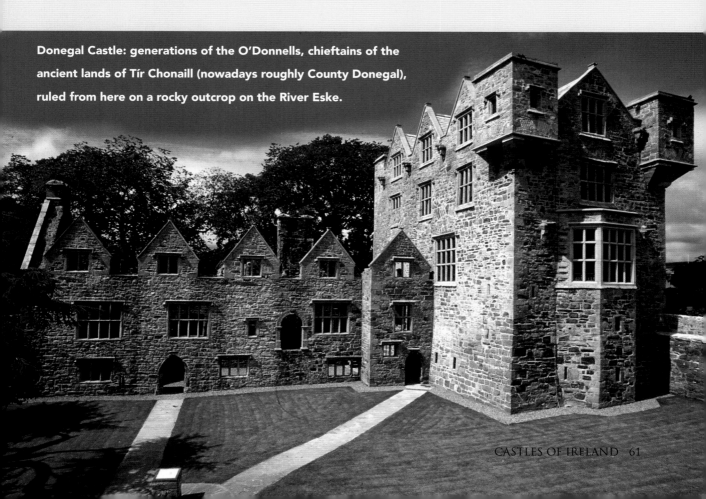

Donegal Castle: generations of the O'Donnells, chieftains of the ancient lands of Tír Chonaill (nowadays roughly County Donegal), ruled from here on a rocky outcrop on the River Eske.

DONEGAL CASTLE

Donegal Castle was one of many O'Donnell strongholds; it is likely that the most famous member of that family, Red Hugh (1572–1602), spent some of his short and tragic life here as a child. In Red Hugh's day, only the tower-house stood here, built by an earlier Red Hugh in the 15th century. Following the Ulster Plantations, the castle came into the hands of Captain Basil Brooke and he changed the old tower-house and built on a fine new gabled manor-house. The main chamber on the first floor was turned into a banqueting hall and two fireplaces, one very large and imposing, were installed.

Red Hugh's Scottish mother, Iníon Dubh, was one of the most formidable characters in Ulster and it was she who arranged for Red Hugh to be fostered by MacSweeney Doe. He was betrothed to Róis, daughter of Hugh O'Neill, Earl of Tyrone, a power balance which caused great consternation to the English Lord Deputy, Sir John Perrot, who had Red Hugh kidnapped at the age of 15 and imprisoned in Dublin Castle, from where he famously escaped.

NEARBY:
The ruins of the Franciscan Friary, founded by Red Hugh O'Donnell I in 1474. An obelisk in the middle of the Diamond commemorates the Four Masters, who compiled the great Annals of Ireland in 1632–36.

DOE CASTLE

Situated on a tiny peninsula of land, and surrounded by the sweeping waters of Sheephaven Bay in north Donegal, Doe Castle consists of a four-storey tower, surrounded by a high-walled bawn. The name Doe (from the Irish *na dtuath* = 'of the territories') was a title applied to the lands of one branch of the MacSweeney family, originally Scottish settlers who were lords of the area and built the castle, probably in the early 16th century. During the disastrous defeat of the Spanish Armada in 1588, a few ships made a landing here and the occupants were given refuge in Doe Castle. It was while in fosterage here that Red Hugh O'Donnell was kidnapped in 1587 on the orders of the Queen's Deputy, Lord Perrott, on board ship at Rathmullan on Lough Swilly. The castle was lost and regained by the MacSweeneys a number of times over the next two centuries.

NEARBY:
Rathmullan, the scene of Red Hugh's kidnapping in 1587 and the Flight of the Earls in 1607.

THE LAKELANDS OF BREIFNE & FERMANAGH

THE ANCIENT TERRITORIES OF BREIFNE (MORE OR LESS
PRESENT-DAY CAVAN, LEITRIM AND PART OF SLIGO), RULED
BY THE O'ROURKES, THE O'REILLYS AND THE MACDERMOTTS,
ALONG WITH FERMANAGH UNDER THE MAGUIRES, FENDED OFF
THE COLONISTS FOR CENTURIES FROM THE LAKES, DRUMLINS
AND FORESTS OF THE REGION. IT WAS ONLY WITH THE
PLANTATION OF ULSTER THAT THE IRISH
LANDS WERE SUBDUED.

Parke's Castle lies on the shores of beautiful Lough Gill. A small island on this same lake inspired
the great poet WB Yeats to pen the well-loved poem 'The Lake Isle of Innisfree'.

PARKE'S CASTLE

An O'Rourke tower-house stood by the shores of Lough Gill until the 16th century. The chieftain Brian O'Rourke gave refuge to Francisco de Cuéllar, a survivor of the disastrous defeat of the Spanish Armada in 1588, who wrote a remarkable account of his wanderings.

By the end of the Elizabethan Wars, Ireland was thoroughly subjugated; proud chieftains like the O'Rourkes were no more and the Ulster Plantation brought new settlers here to occupy their confiscated lands. Captain Robert Parke made his way as far as Lough Gill, demolished the O'Rourke tower-house (remains of which came to light during excavations in the 1970s) and built this stronghouse which bears his name.

NEARBY:

The beauty of Yeats Country in County Sligo and the Crockauns/Keelogyboy Bogs Natural Heritage Area on the border with County Leitrim.

ENNISKILLEN CASTLE

The Water Gate in Enniskillen is a pleasant stopping-off point for locals and visitors alike, situated as it is in the beautiful Lough Erne lakeland. Its centrepiece is the building which houses Fermanagh County Museum today. Here, at a strategic location at the head of Lower Lough Erne, Hugh Maguire, chieftain of Fermanagh, built a tower-house and bawn in 1415. It was the principal seat of the Maguires, and an important focus of Irish resistance to the English. The castle we see today is later, the work of the Planter Captain William Cole, who was granted the Maguire territory in the 17th century. The base of the old Maguire tower-house is incorporated in the keep. The two rounded bartizans of the Watergate are Scottish architectural features introduced by Cole.

NEARBY:

The monastic sites of Devenish Island.

MONEA

Not far from Enniskillen is the picturesquely situated Monea. This Planter castle is three storeys high and stands in a bawn. The two towers carry square caphouses, which are a Scottish architectural feature.

TULLY

Tully Castle was the scene of a terrible massacre on Christmas Day 1641. Built by one Lord Hume in the territory of the dispossessed Maguires, the castle was besieged during the 1641 Rebellion and surrendered to Rory Maguire on Christmas Eve on condition of safe conduct for some of the local Protestant settlers who had taken refuge there. Tragically, 69 women and children and 16 men were massacred by the Maguires on the following day.

Another Plantation castle, Tully, on the shores of Lower Lough Erne, has beautifully restored gardens with plants known in Ireland in the 17th century.

A tiny island just off the shore of Lough Oughter holds the circular castle of Clogh Oughter, weighed down with history.

CLOGH OUGHTER

For those visiting the beautiful Killykeen Forest Park in County Cavan, the castle known as Clogh Oughter can be reached by boat across Lough Oughter. The original Irish name of the castle was *Cloch Locha Uachtair*, which means 'the stone castle in the lake'.

The castle was a Norman stronghold, built in the O'Reilly territory of East Breifne around 1220 by the de Lacys. Before long, it was captured by the local chieftain, 'Crannóg' O'Reilly, and for the next 400 years or so, it stayed mainly in O'Reilly hands. A place of strategic importance, it weathered many dramatic events during the course of its history. During the 1641 Rebel-lion, local Protestant settlers were imprisoned here by the O'Reillys and one who languished for some weeks here was William Bedell, the Protestant Bishop of Kilmore. *Bedell's Bible*, as it is known, is a translation into Irish of the Old Testament, which he commissioned.

According to tradition, Clogh Oughter was where the untimely and tragic death (proba-bly by poison) of the great leader Owen Roe O'Neill took place in 1649, as he prepared to move against Cromwell. This much-lamented event was followed by the Cromwellian siege of the castle in 1653, after which the castle was peacefully surrendered.

THE NORTH-EAST

THE FERTILE PASTURES AND STRATEGIC COASTLINES OF DOWN
AND ANTRIM MUST HAVE SEEMED LIKE A GREAT PRIZE WHEN
THE REGION WAS INVADED BY THE ANGLO-NORMANS UNDER
JOHN DE COURCY IN 1177. A SERIES OF MOTTE AND BAILEYS
WERE EARLY STRONG POINTS, FROM WHICH THEY CONTROLLED
THE COUNTRYSIDE. HOWEVER, THEIR SETTLEMENT WAS
SHORTLIVED AND RESTRICTED EVENTUALLY TO A FEW COASTAL
ENCLAVES AND THE AREA WAS DOMINATED BY THE GAELIC
OVERLORDS, THE MAGENNISES OF THE CLAN AODH.

Built by Hugh de Lacy, Greencastle, along with
King John's Castle at Carlingford, commands
the narrow entry to Carlingford Lough.

GREENCASTLE

By the shores of Carlingford Lough, the ruined curtain-walls with four corner towers enclose the large rectangular keep of Greencastle. For many years, in August, the green by the castle bore witness to a strange sight as the 'Ram Fair' took place and a great ram was brought to the top of the castle and placed upon a throne.

KILCLIEF CASTLE

Kilclief Castle (below), situated beside a quiet bay 4km (2½m) south of Strangford, is an early tower-house dating from 1413. Bishop John Sely lived here and was sacked in 1441 for his scandalous behaviour in living with Lettice Thomas, a married woman.

DUNDRUM CASTLE

Dundrum Castle (right) is on an imposing hilltop overlooking the bay of the same name and was begun by John de Courcy shortly after he invaded Ulster in 1177. You can climb to the very top of this great circular keep and see the fine views.

STRANGFORD CASTLE

Strangford Lough was guarded at its entrance by the 16th-century Strangford Castle, and Portaferry across the lough had its own tower-house too.

NARROW WATER CASTLE

Narrow Water Castle (below) is a well-preserved tower-house, strategically situated on the shore of Carlingford Lough, close to Warrenpoint. Built in the 1560s as an English garrison, it later fell into the hands of the Magennises.

Audley's Castle is the focus of a beautiful vista along the waters of Strangford Lough.

JORDAN'S CASTLE

Jordan's Castle (above), in the centre of the lovely medieval town and port of Ardglass, is a tower-house dating from the 15th century.

AUDLEY'S CASTLE

This 15th-century tower-house was built by the Audleys and is similar to Kilclief with its high arch machicolation over the main entrance, linking two towers. A relatively comfortable home, the tower has several garderobes, window-seats and cupboards. It passed to the Wards in 1646.

DUNLUCE

The *Dún* in the name suggests the presence of an early fortification such as a promontory-fort here. There is a *souterrain* (an early medieval underground passage) underneath the ruins. The great circular towers on the eastern side suggest a date in the 14th century, but most of the rest of the buildings are believed to be from the 16th and early 17th centuries. A wooden bridge where a drawbridge formerly hung conveys us from the outer courtyard across a deep chasm to the gatehouse with its corbelled turrets. Much of the original paving survives and the ruin of the great hall dominates the yard.

Little is known of the history of the castle itself before the 16th century when it was in the hands of the MacQuillans, who were displaced by the MacDonnells, 'Lords of the Isles' and rulers of vast estates on the west coast of Scotland. Dunluce had no shortage of dramatic episodes over the centuries. The most colourful of the MacDonnells was Sorley Boy MacDonnell (Somhairle Buí, *buí* = yellow-haired), who twice lost the castle, once to Shane O'Neill and in 1584 to Sir John Perrott, the Queen's Deputy in Ireland. Sorley Boy regained the castle, however, and repairs were underway when he died in 1589. The wreck of the *Girona*, a ship of the Spanish Armada, came aground here in 1588 and cannon retrieved at the time were mounted on gun-ports in the curtain wall.

Dunluce was a place of great grandeur in the 1600s when Randal MacDonnell, the second Earl of Antrim, and his wife, Lady Katherine,

On the Antrim coast Dunluce is the most spectacularly situated castle in the whole of Ireland.

were in charge. The Earl had spent much of his youth at the English court as a guarantee of his father's loyalty and was close to Charles I, as was Katherine, one of the richest women in England. There are accounts of lavish furnishings, tapestries, mirrors and all the trappings of a rich and powerful family. The ruins of a grand two-storey hall in the yard with three mullioned bay windows and service rooms beyond suggest a great household. In 1639 part of the lower yard fell into the sea, bringing several members of the household with it.

In keeping with the instability of life in the 17th century, the Earl was arrested in 1642 during the Irish Rebellion. The contents of the castle were shipped to England for safe-keeping, but were dispersed by the Cromwellian government. The castle was deserted and fell into ruin, although it remained the property of the Earls of Antrim until 1928.

The splendid castle of Carrickfergus is an imposing stronghold on a rocky promontory standing guard over Belfast Lough.

The big, brightly lit room on the fourth storey of Carrickfergus Castle, with windows on all sides and a fireplace, was the living area for de Courcy and his family.

CARRICKFERGUS CASTLE

Carrickfergus Castle was begun by the Norman adventurer John de Courcy, who marched into east Ulster in 1177, and the massive keep along with the inner ward were probably built by him. The four-storey keep has all the features of a medieval stronghold with its gloomy entrance, a large dimly lit room without a fireplace and visitors will also see the deep well and the huge vaulted cellars.

De Courcy's tenure was shortlived as he was ousted in 1204 by Hugh de Lacy (son of de Lacy who built Trim). He in turn was expelled by King John on his visit to Ireland in 1210, who thought such a great fortress would suit nicely as a garrison in this strategic spot. A further defensive wall was built around 1220 and by the middle of the century, the outer ward and the gatehouse had been built, taking in the entire rocky promontory. Carrickfergus was the Crown's principal administrative centre in Ulster throughout the later Middle Ages.

LIVING IN A CASTLE/ TOWER-HOUSE

Castles were always bustling with life and with the owner acting as protector to neighbouring families, many of them worked for him guarding the property, herding the animals, or living with the family as household servants.

Most castles were surrounded by a bawn, or walled enclosure (*bán* comes from *bó-dhún* which means something like 'cow-fortress'), which often had several buildings within its walls along with gardens and a large building known as the Hall for entertaining.

In earlier castles an open fire burned in the middle of the top floor, or two, as chimneys generally only came to be built in the 16th century. The main cooking was often carried out in another building outside in the bawn. Light would have come from tallow candles, or torches, on the walls. The walls and floors were covered in animal skins and straw for warmth.

Only the very grandest establishments had imported tapestries and rugs.

Guests were entertained in these rooms with feasting, singing and storytelling. Great hospitality was part of the Irish way of life.

Bedrooms were often shared by many members of the family; privacy as we know it today was nonexistent. Servants and guards would have slept near the fires, or wherever they found a spot to lay their heads.

Rooms in castles tended to be rather dark as the windows were narrow slits from which arrows could be fired. The inside of the window had an embrasure or a space wide enough to allow the longbow man some elbow room to load his arrows. Mullioned windows came in when arrows went out of use and these were wider and gave more light. Many castles have musket-holes for firing guns through from the 16th century onwards.

A machicolation was an overhanging piece of wall with an opening underneath through which stones or other missiles would be thrown. Bartizans were similar but overlooked the corners of buildings.

The top of the castle was the safest place to be, so the main living area for the owner and his family was in the large rooms on the top one or two storeys.

The base of the castle walls was splayed out or 'battered' so that the flying missiles bounced off the base, causing further damage.

The entire first floor was generally a guards' room, which gave access to the stairs.

The spiral staircase was always built in a clockwise direction, so that a right-handed defender could wield his sword on the way down.

All castles were built with defensive features. Any intruder would have had to watch out approaching a castle. First of all there was the moat. A moat was a deep ditch surrounding the castle, dug out of the bedrock and usually filled with water. They tended to be part of early important castles. Dublin Castle famously had a moat and you can see the remains of one today at Ferns. Then there might have been a portcullis, which is a massive iron gate on a pulley system with sharp iron teeth located over the main gateway to a castle. Roscrea and Cahir both have their portcullis machinery restored. All comings and goings would have been observed from the battlements, which had machicolations.

The main entrance was often on the first floor and just overhead was the murder-hole, through which intruders who had made it this far would have been pelted with rocks or other missiles.

LOCATION INDEX & MAP

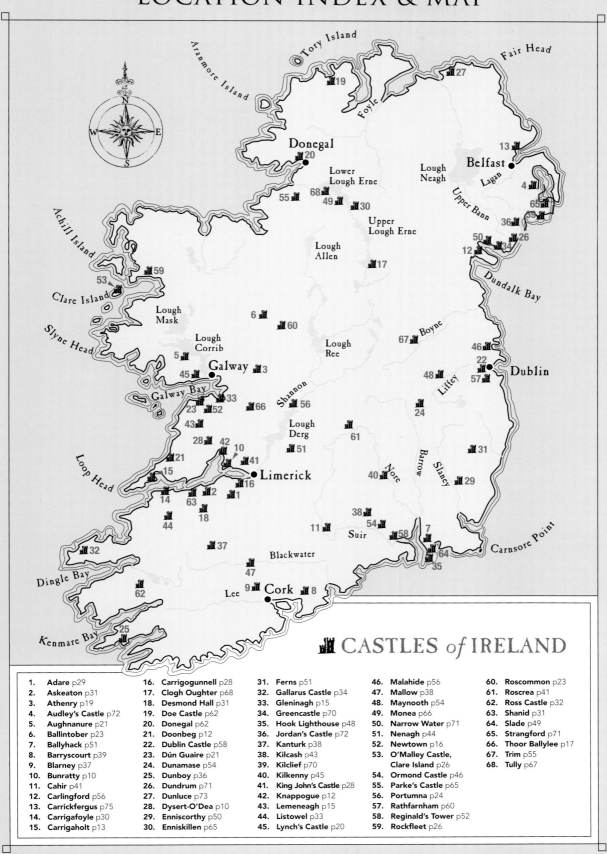

Tory Island
19
27 Fair Head
Aranmore Island
Foyle
Donegal 20
Lower Lough Erne
13
Belfast
Lough Neagh
Lagan
4
55 68 49 30 Upper Lough Erne
65
36
50 26
12 34
Lough Allen 17
Dundalk Bay
Achill Island
53 59
Clare Island
Slyne Head
Lough Mask
6 60
Boyne
67
46
Lough Corrib
5 45 3 Galway
Shannon
Lough Ree
22 Dublin
57
48 Liffey
23 52 33 66 56
43
28 42 10 Lough Derg
21 15 41 61 24 31
16 Limerick 51
2 Nore Barrow Slaney
14 63 40 29
18 44 Loop Head
38
32 11 54 58 7
37 Suir 64
47 Blackwater 35
62 9 Cork 8 Carnsore Point
Lee
25 Kenmare Bay
Dingle Bay

CASTLES of IRELAND

1. **Adare** p29	16. **Carrigogunnell** p28	31. **Ferns** p51	46. **Malahide** p56	60. **Roscommon** p23
2. **Askeaton** p31	17. **Clogh Oughter** p68	32. **Gallarus Castle** p34	47. **Mallow** p38	61. **Roscrea** p41
3. **Athenry** p19	18. **Desmond Hall** p31	33. **Gleninagh** p15	48. **Maynooth** p54	62. **Ross Castle** p32
4. **Audley's Castle** p72	19. **Doe Castle** p62	34. **Greencastle** p70	49. **Monea** p66	63. **Shanid** p31
5. **Aughnanure** p21	20. **Donegal** p62	35. **Hook Lighthouse** p48	50. **Narrow Water** p71	64. **Slade** p49
6. **Ballintober** p23	21. **Doonbeg** p12	36. **Jordan's Castle** p72	51. **Nenagh** p44	65. **Strangford** p71
7. **Ballyhack** p51	22. **Dublin Castle** p58	37. **Kanturk** p38	52. **Newtown** p16	66. **Thoor Ballylee** p17
8. **Barryscourt** p39	23. **Dún Guaire** p21	38. **Kilcash** p43	53. **O'Malley Castle,**	67. **Trim** p55
9. **Blarney** p37	24. **Dunamase** p54	39. **Kilclief** p70	**Clare Island** p26	68. **Tully** p67
10. **Bunratty** p10	25. **Dunboy** p36	40. **Kilkenny** p45	54. **Ormond Castle** p46	
11. **Cahir** p41	26. **Dundrum** p71	41. **King John's Castle** p28	55. **Parke's Castle** p65	
12. **Carlingford** p56	27. **Dunluce** p73	42. **Knappogue** p12	56. **Portumna** p24	
13. **Carrickfergus** p75	28. **Dysert-O'Dea** p10	43. **Lemeneagh** p15	57. **Rathfarnham** p60	
14. **Carrigafoyle** p30	29. **Enniscorthy** p50	44. **Listowel** p33	58. **Reginald's Tower** p52	
15. **Carrigaholt** p13	30. **Enniskillen** p65	45. **Lynch's Castle** p20	59. **Rockfleet** p26	

First published 2007 by The O'Brien Press Ltd,

12 Terenure Road East, Rathgar, Dublin 6, D06 HD27, Ireland.

Tel: +353 1 4923333; Fax: +353 1 4922777

E-mail: books@obrien.ie. Website: www.obrien.ie

The O'Brien Press is a member of Publishing Ireland.

This edition first published 2015.

Reprinted 2017.

ISBN: 978-1-84717-667-7

7 6 5 4 3 2

21 20 19 18 17

Printed and bound in Poland by Białostockie Zakłady Graficzne S.A.
The paper in this book is produced using pulp from managed forests

Picture credits:

Front cover image: Emma Byrne. Back cover: Kilkenny & Trim (Emmet McLaughlin); Monea, Clogh Oughter & Dunluce (Irish Image Collection); Barryscourt (Department of Environment, Heritage and Culture); Hook (Emma Byrne); Blarney (Ben Russell). Mairéad Ashe FitzGerald: p12 (bottom); Emma Byrne: pp18, 48, 49, 51 (top); Emmet McLaughlin: pp20 (top), 45 (top), 47, 50, 52, 55 (top), 56, 57 (bottom), 71 (bottom); Department of Environment, Heritage and Culture: pp5, 9, 11, 14, 19, 20 (bottom), 22, 24, 27, 29, 30 (bottom), 31, 32, 38, 39, 40, 43, 45 (inset), 46, 53, 58, 60, 61, 64; Clare County Library: pp7, 13; Clare County Library/Sue and Roger Diel: pp15, 16; Michael Diggin: pp33, 34; Chris Hill@scenicireland.com: p51 (bottom); Ben Russell: pp35, 36, 37; Dublin Tourism: p57 (top); Irish Image Collection: pp17, 25, 63, 67, 69, 71 (top), 72 (bottom), 73, 75; Shannon Heritage: pp12 (top), 21; Shutterstock: p26; Robert Vance: pp6, 23 (both), 42, 44, 54, 59, 66, 67, 70, 72 (top), 74; drawings taken from *Pacata Hibernia* Vols I & II. Illustrations by Uto Hogerzeil: pp55 (inset), 77, 78.

The author and publisher have endeavoured to establish the origin of all images used. If any involuntary infringement of copyright has occurred, sincere apologies are offered and the owners are requested to contact the publishers.